Contents

Good for you

Everyone needs to eat the right kind of food to stay healthy. The food we eat comes from plants and animals.

A healthy meal is made up of fresh fruit and vegetables with some meat.

4

GOOD FOOD

Popcorn

Meat, Fish and Eggs

Julia Adams

Explore the world with **Popcorn** – your complete first non-fiction library.

Look out for more titles in the Popcorn range. All books have the same format of simple text and striking images. Text is carefully matched to the pictures to help readers to identify and understand key vocabulary.
www.waylandbooks.co.uk/popcorn

First published in 2010 by Wayland
This paperback edition published in 2012 by Wayland

Wayland
Hachette Children's Books
338 Euston Road
London NW1 3BH

Wayland Australia
Level 17/207 Kent Street
Sydney NSW 2000

Editor: Julia Adams
Designer: Paul Cherrill
Picture Researcher: Julia Adams
Food and Nutrition Consultant: Ester Davies
Photo models: Asha Francis; Lydia Washbourne

British Library Cataloguing in Publication Data
Adams, Julia.
   Meat, fish and eggs. -- (Popcorn. Good food)
   1. Proteins in human nutrition--Juvenile literature.
   2. Food of animal origin--Juvenile literature.
   I. Title II. Series
   641.3'06-dc22

ISBN 978 0 7502 6759 5

Wayland is a division of Hachette Children's Books,
an Hachette UK company, www.hachette.co.uk

Photographs:

Alamy: Juniors Bildarchiv / F300 7, Gari Wyn Williams 8, Daniel Hurst / Editorial 9, Chris Gomersall 10, Mira 11, mediablitzimages (uk) Limited 14, FLPA 18; Andy Crawford: 12, 15, 22, 23; Corbis: Ariel Skelley 13; Getty: Tara Moore OFC/5; Shutterstock: Monkey Business Images 1/4, 6, 19; AVAVA 2/21, PeJo 16, Palabra 17, Goran Kuzmanovski 20;

Meat, fish and eggs are good
foods because they have protein.
This helps your body grow.

A boiled egg and toast for
breakfast is a healthy way
to start the day.

Food from animals

The meat we eat comes from animals, such as cows, sheep and chickens. There are also many types of fish that we can eat.

Lean chicken with vegetables is good for you and tasty, too.

We eat other food from animals as well. Yoghurt and cheese are made of cow's milk.

The eggs we eat are laid by chickens.

Farming

Most animals whose meat we eat are kept on farms. They spend some time outside during the day.

At night, farm animals sleep in a pen, like these pigs.

Chickens live in a coop. They lay
their eggs in a nest. Many chickens
are kept together and they
sometimes share a nest.

We eat eggs that have been
collected from chickens' nests.

Fishing

Fish live in water. Some fish, such as cod and tuna, live in the seas and oceans. Fishermen sail out to sea in big boats to catch them with nets.

Why do you think these seagulls are flying around this fishing boat?

Other fish, like salmon and trout, live in rivers and lakes. Some of these fish are kept in big pools of water, called fish farms.

This is a fish farm in Idaho, USA.

Poultry

The meat that comes from chickens and turkey is called poultry. This meat is pink in colour. The skin is white.

These are the legs and a thigh of a chicken.

The legs of a chicken are called drumsticks. Why do you think this is?

We fry, roast or boil poultry to eat it. We can add it to stir-fries, pasta dishes, soups and curries.

At Christmas, many people have roast turkey.

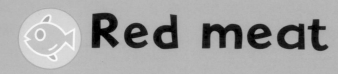

Red meat

Meat that comes from cows, pigs and sheep is called red meat. This name comes from the meat's colour.

This meat is from the ribs of a cow. Can you see the rib bones?

Pig's meat is called pork. We make sausages, ham and bacon from pork. Meat from cows is called beef.

The minced meat in bolognaise sauce is made from beef.

The meat from an adult sheep is called mutton.

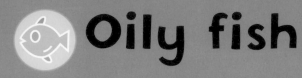 Oily fish

We eat the flesh of fish. The flesh also contains fish oil. Some types of fish have more fish oil than others. We call them oily fish. Tuna, salmon and herring are all oily fish.

These tuna fish have just been caught from the sea.

Fish oil helps to keep our heart
and brain healthy. Oily fish can
be baked, grilled or fried.

Salmon is pink. Can you see it on these skewers?

White fish

Cod, haddock and pollock are white fish because their flesh is white. They live in seas, oceans, lakes and rivers.

These haddock have just been caught at sea. The ice keeps them fresh.

We eat white fish in many dishes.
Fish and chips, fish fingers and
most fish cakes are all made with
white fish.

We use pollock, haddock or
cod to make fish and chips.

 # Eggs

Eggs have a hard shell. Inside, they are made up of egg white and yolk.

The yolk is the yellow part in the middle of the egg. It is surrounded by egg white.

When eggs are raw, the egg white is clear. It turns white when the egg is cooked.

You can boil, scramble or fry eggs.
We also use eggs to make foods,
such as mayonnaise and meringue.

We often use
eggs to bake
cakes.

Make a cheese and ham sandwich

You will need:
- two slices of bread
- butter • lettuce leaves
- one tomato • ham slices
- cheese • a knife
- kitchen roll

Try making this tasty sandwich for lunch.

1. Spread butter on one side of each slice of bread.

2. Ask an adult to help you cut three or four slices of cheese. Place them on a slice of bread.

3. Lay a few slices of ham on the cheese.

22

4. Wash the tomato and a few lettuce leaves. Use some kitchen roll to dry them.

5. Lay the lettuce leaves on the ham. Ask an adult to help you slice the tomato.

6. Place the tomato slices on the lettuce and cover with the other slice of bread. Cut your sandwich in half. Enjoy!

Glossary

coop a place where chickens lay their eggs on a farm

fish farms places where fish are kept in big pools

lean something that has very little or no fat

protein a substance in food that helps our bodies grow

raw not cooked

thigh the part of the leg between the knee and the hip

Index